Aerial Concave Without Cloud

Aerial Concave Without Cloud

Sueyeun Juliette Lee 이수연

Nightboat Books
New York

Printed in the United States

ISBN: 978-1-64362-116-6

Cover photograph: *Red Star* by Jake Sigl
Interior photographs by Sueyeun Juliette Lee
Design and typesetting by Somnath Bhatt and Rissa Hochberger
Typeset in Alegreya Regular, Akkurat Pro and Adobe Myungjo Std.

Cataloging-in-publication data is available from the Library of Congress

Nightboat Books
New York
www.nightboat.org

Table of Contents

To enclose light is to prepare the way for life.

—Gaston Bachelard

the appropriate information in the negative

part of the ensuing discourse about light
was written at my desire
to comprehend the phenomenon
through the lens of my
breathing body

I have here publish'd
what I think proper to come abroad

in all languages
with my consent

I am not yet satisfied about it
for want of experiments

at the end I have added
some questions

it was easy to form mental pictures
of waves and particles

easy to make certain kinds of predictions
concerning the probable results of future observations
which remained logically consistent
and frequently very useful

yet this picture may be unsuited to describe
certain other types of observations

we must admit that the results
of our experiments on light are
in some ways
different from the results of observation
in its transformation of
a visual encounter with the world
into a "memorable" ___________

the meaning of these words
are derived from the experiments
which they describe
we must not deduce
the truth of light
all that we can say is

(different characteristics and capabilities

consider the entire process in
a unified manner from the start

a complex and fluid medium
light enters ultimately
at the intuitive level
merging into a single coherent function
more commonly recognized as *life*

with practice may we become proficient
within this amber dark calling[1]

by trial and error methods
usually "normal" or with luck
may I achieve otherwise
which pleases me

when I began I found
I worked
I was aware of the danger
of parroting light yet
I proceed

---

1 *to see*

it was obvious to me that
there must be some bridge
a basic theory in the medium
a creative means for
unveiling the blindness
figurative within
it is essential to translate arcane principles[2]
into an applied craft
out of this may
we all be reformed
in negative
in negative blue

---

2 *comparable to the preparation of a weather map without a central meteorological station*

there was considerable skepticism
prior developments were purely technical[3]
they sometimes contradicted
the sensitive trajectory within me
like physical branches
embraced and scorned
am I flexible enough to be adapted
which now leads me to this work
asking how I otherwise maintain conventions

(to distinguish the luminous qualities[4]
the limits of the real

such refinements perhaps
in no way alter
our basic concepts)

---

3 *am I forever indebted // precarious invasion of accepted procedures*
4 *an approach*

who is concerned
with this broad spectrum day
housed so neatly
in the blood's awareness
there is today a severe gulf
in daylight
the trend is to produce casual
contributions over
acute precisions which are
also unsophisticated

no fail-safe provisions

am I grateful when
"progress" interferes with creative excellence
or distressed

it has been said at various times
however that the advent of such
vehicles for thought and certain materials
obviate our need for insight
reflecting a misconception
as it occurs in the central value
of the human body[5]

a further misconception emphasizes
craft at the expense of
human longing

---

5 *if they change do we discard them, too* ((subject // luminous

assume an expanse
in the imagination
observe
no limitations
functional or poetic

be prepared to replace
what no longer applies
though the basic principle remains

(life

the variations that have evolved
are perhaps recognizable

make an effort to understand
eagerly await the blue light
its next major “advance”

inherent with inescapable structural characteristics
true ________ demands no shortcuts
tricks or formulas
a comprehensive vision
which is common to
the blood’s memory
massive cloud of
radiant harmonic delay

하지
夏至

a tree

> the distant trees in the mist must have sufficient “body”
> but the mist must remain
>
> —Ansel Adams

> the familiar tree, the being with no face,
>
> —Gaston Bachelard

luminous peri-solar accord
in various and greenly
speaks flight to earth
ascent and deep

to duplicate such brightnesses
hold that light inside your mind
become aware of its
expressive intention before completed
a conscious intuitive experience

“tree”

that tree—

such subjective
"departures from reality"
shine gold and sway
rattling soft clarion
against my body's wall

far from a literal transcriptive actuality
create “the emotional equivalent

now in one dimension

black and white

                                but green

silvered dehiscences
motivating a total
vehicular impression

can one ever
a single, an only, a one
a tree

minus blue

in aerial work
sometimes one
explanation
is more complicated
than the other

for the sake of
clear description
unfold the terminal
blue

clouds and sky
are important
luminescence
an absolute quantity

penetrate the general
atmospheric haze

observe
in sharp detail
more generous gradients

expire

in deep blue
and nothing
no empty shadow

refute
the blank
white sky

the incident

a narrow band
to which one is sensitive
beyond which lies the invisible
some is inevitably lost

how so?

to fall is a great incident
to fall slowly
without injury
is to become a magnitude
in reckoning

all things fall
“gracefully”
are you grateful
for what has fallen
into you

standard // average // common
all integrated in the single reading

to make a record
one must capture
what is reflected
evaluating what one wants
to be represented

in counterclockwise rotation, arms outstretched, feel the sun's hard blue descent into the black coal of your breathing body. gather without reflection. gather infinitely, growing fine as a needle's spray along the skin. surmise the quality of infinite duration, flexing intimate storms into apparel. all dark scintillation, honed.

I sought to uncover my primary mother's body firstly by standing alone on the basalt shore. All gleamed with a crystalline equanimity. Stark blue light coursed upwards with suspension as a slow heat dissolved into my pores. Flexing the long stones inside my legs as mass, I moved with a deliberate, calculated pace towards the shore.

that which travels from one place to another
interacting with matter can be transformed
it would be incomplete
or the law would fail
if the transfers and transformations
were not accounted for

no exact correspondences
an approximation

“to form a descriptive system appropriate, with minor modifications, to a wide range of observations in sound and light, as well as to waves

can a body be indifferent
to the incident, to
all common properties
that disturb

“by its use certain important results are obtained in a simple way

I would like
to speak simply

“you

Bleached convoy, my words flutter on no flag. Without fire, they relinquish their missives reflectively, casting in negative an old fury now quelled into a neutral desire to simply "see": to recover what conjured forth a name.

some is inevitably lost

(

bow slowly and rise, transforming the crown of the head into a vertical suspiration. strive to announce a perfectly quiet reception in the limbs, now steadfastly affirmed by their polar coordination. find purchase in the dark curling swarm that were once toes.

if the disturbance has a scalar quantity
if the disturbance produces a similar disturbance at a neighboring point
at a slightly later time
if the disturbance is continuously transformed from one place to another

what is neglected in the present discussion
strive to determine the initial conditions
flower into what must hold

neon rain, phosphorescence (tears

what are we doing to each other
in the surplus fog
a mutual touch becomes
a myriad condition
in which all feelings sleep

open the windows
in the room where I lay
protesting the notion
that coherent sources of light are
always images of one original source

let me interrogate arctic bees about
the stark quadrants they tumble over
how they convert glacial suffering
into sunburned drinkable dew—

such *apparent* brightnesses

this is a complex and profound
physiological capability
that has no counterpart

the shadowed areas take
on an elevated brightness
shapes and textures come to life
in the dark soil of a humming body

what could we experience
of the luminous world
forsaking ourselves
to permanent noon

clouds

rich
massive opalescences

of moderate exaggeration

it is always a surprise
to see the same clouds appear

clouds often lighted by the sun

you cannot expect to hold
the entirety

a major distortion can always
destroy the impression
of light

how to keep that
appearance

delicate translucency
(no marked degree

is the sky obvious
is it even
what value is the sky
nearby

:

give more consideration
to the clouds

accept the shadow's value
as essential
against the threshold
of the negative

chalk-white
shapeless mass or
dead, gray

manage the information
produce good variations
there is no empty shadow
intention is always
gently luminous

I find it hard
to say goodbye
to clouds

shoreless sea of fluctuating fire

the least light or part
which may be stopp'd alone without the rest
do suffer   *(any thing alone*

I call a ray

fields of purest aether
transparent forms, too fine for mortal sight
thin glitt'ring textures of the filmy dew
the whitening undistinguished blaze
in a bright cloud aspires

what dyes the rose; what paints the heavn'ly bow
a wide, a various, and a glittering flame
bright effluence
by myriads forth at once
swarming they pour
a trembling variance of revolving hues
infinite source
of beauty, ever flushing, ever new
aerial concave without cloud

for that part of
which is stopp'd
cannot be the same
with that which is let pass
propagated in time

I have chosen to agree

o unprofuse magnificence divine
o wisdom truly perfect
prime cheerer
soul of surrounding worlds
efflux divine
in white promise forth

the invisible *latent image*
the nature
the time
the amount of agitation

any remaining trace
~~must be eliminated~~

I remind you that what we see is
the effect of the light passing through
in translucent folds
to “breathe”

lamp of day
still flaming with full ardor
a dazzling deluge reigns
wide the pale deluge floats
of silver radiance
lavish of lustre
that subtile spirit
its copious mantle spreads
over the wide-extended universe

simple
the former light
I call *primary*

the aerial nature of celestial blue

what comes to life
with the smallest cloud
in solidified blue
suffers an enormous loss

such is life for
the blue sky in a wildflower
or blue eyes at dusk

that distant blue infinity
rises sternly in the soul
vibrates in no sonorous crystal
tonalizes only in the
swift muscular engine
we call clarity, not day

concourse of correspondences
limned with blue hands
active in its dynamics
of dematerialization

dream after the finesse of ancient galleries
whose calm hallways in infinite attention
remain, counseling

a possessed good
such a minimum of substance
in which the bell rings
of its own accord

동지
冬至

a pale saturation (in day

in *none* light
in a swarm of gray and descent
in a charmed haze
into that dissipating fabric—
hail yourself to the sky
  ephemeral, isolate
  ever without peer

after black seahorses drop from your pale body
after you've tasted that bitter well
erased from November
an angry line

"a gray blue storm is slowly rolling in

What do you wish to forget?

Becoming attuned to the monaural surround drives you to dehisce into the arctic pale above, mirrored in a traceless horizon. This space "of blue" eats up the limits of the human body—my organs coalesce instead as a slow pulse of asymmetrical gray light.

In deep saturation and swarm, in this ultramarine aeriality. What storm.

Breathe lightly across my face. My cheeks are already languid floes across my features. Peer into me with the warmest winter ice I have never touched.

to reach

“yet the bones cry otherwise

The spatial constant of cold requires a renewed commitment to dignity.

With grace, stride into the crisp churn of snow roses. How blown into translucent integrity, a fact. To survive, flesh cries "take hold and kneel," the way blue lakes and horses without shadows or the memory of a distant lawn—

The body cries: *a mother—*

Does it root. Does it squint into the slate baseline under this valley's head.
Sky summons otherwise, to lose all and fathom. Like smoke.

I see invariably across all the years when I transcribe the intensity of your gaze.

The approximate lesson: no hold. None.
And as one forgets, walk.

In gray light and wind, the inconstant quarreling turn of it over absent walls.
Then a sudden sleet, shifting. Am I alone.

The pressure of it—the atmosphere here is an intensity of small children,
their insistence.

Do you continue to give into it?
What else do you long for?

as a posture
as a possibility
as black basalt then bud

spring, such
a pale saturation
(in day

to become properly aerial
alert the “tree” inside you
how it dematerializes and
snowy noise
darting narrow cinders of my attention
in gray blue
then white

speak that infinite word
a method of ignition
without confusion
or pain

continually
don't break open
keep leaning into
give

the thaw

> The thawe began this yeare... at which time there began to
> spring up...
> a certain stragling grasse, with a blewish flower
> —Robert Fotherby

an extensive white monotony
breaks infrequently
into a black rock ridge
stark sable spleen

it is a land
with and without
people

cleft by ice wedges
cutting secretive black soil polygonally—
note this labor to press them outward
how all arranges their clinging misery
softly

water transforms *forcefully*
engage the scree
interior to your complexion

neither too thin nor grim
but plentiful and
far from the case

dovekies wheel and circle
above the frozen sea

the loss is distributed across sinuous silhouettes
combed over in hoarfrost before the whiteout descends

now bend—
lacking polarized lenses
to orient the field of my gaze
all-consumed by blind ambient day

I knelt, a pale coil
((a crisis

*

descend and note
how snow then ice
pulse aqueous green compressed
deeper with enduring force

channel fury through solar induction
drawn down through your common clay
pull pale strength into rigid limbs

converting all

jade then

then blue and further
gravity, blue

with abandon, then drop

now blue

how many realize that the blue-print is almost universally
at the foundation of everything at the present time?

between thaw and frost:

scar the land
tear the roots of plants
bury entire communities
what rubble

the alternations squeeze and move stones
pressing them upward, outward
arranging them
from tail to tide

enter sinew
enter brook
enter far heath
enter fledge
enter fern

enter calcite
enter speleothem
enter marmot
enter tern

enter cirrus
enter talus
enter violet
enter spore
enter saxifrage

enter calix
enter harp seal
enter
but enter

I want to understand what opens up in this dis-attended collection at the periphery of perception, at the seeming limit of its transformation. This incredible *freeze* reemerges to me as an ecological archive for some later, more subtly perceptive intelligences to uncover. In glacial caves, I intuit how the blue ice whorls resound with an oceanic rhythm perhaps also common to light. Its blueness indicates a cold birth, an emergent destiny. I put my open mouth to it, feel millennially ancient ash caught—trapped—in its beveling. *Who speaks?*

Other [exploited] archives ...
owe their significance
to some individuals of
certain species growing at
the margin of their ecological tolerance,
which

without extinction,
brilliantly

sensitively
record
even minor fluctuations

press your hand against the calm spokes of these turns,
awaken the former blue daylight within:
whose beginning
    without category

without sides
indexed into the "far" sky
transfixed above you
those glassy captures
near-motionless waves

as if a curve were a horizon
as if distance remonstrates song
as if each cell were an integer

        an integrated fact of resilient ((light
        through tension, then clarified forms

a lark went trilling up, up into the blue

try to provide any imitation of this sheen or hue

:: ultramarine : azure : cyan ::

identify a molten beat inside the human ruin, with acquiescence
what are you willing to relive
lacking breath, past the cylinders of what you could endure
below the uncurling arctic "sea"
discover the manifesting figure bent gently
in glowing columns of aquatic ice

has shielding the body had any marked influence upon the human organism?

a uniform regulation of the heart's action
increased activity of the skin
fuller and slower respiration
gradually increased respiratory capacity
diminished irritability
all is also concentrated upon the body

light is already serving humanity
its future is promising
the actual intervals
the most powerful destroyers
a light which does not inhibit healing
   (does this kind of energy have value?

spar sight and churn
fragile cyanic glaze

((this question remains unanswered
((the data are inadequate
((systematic work must be done

((order may arise from the present chaos

remagnetized as they touch
magpies fail to make noise
as they settle to the blanched ground

a fair breeze

when the illusion of enveloping light is lost

when shadows fall at a great distance
we must not overlook the subjective importance
of light as a phenomenal encounter

when carried beyond the optimum
opalescent qualities are lost
the main problem is how to retain
the impression of light falling

that feeling of morning light's descent
in a November tumulting sky
has as complex a relationship
as touching her hand in death

in portraiture, eye sockets
should not be overlooked
stark lights fail boundaries
when captured in the finest grades

believe that the sun will rise
into another, obviously

there is no more beautiful illumination
that that from open sky
its intensity may be reduced
and fully appreciated
made eloquent
in terms of the living image
that ratio between sunlit skin
and deep forest shade

light in relation to biological science

the dominant direction of daylight
is from *above*
our basic impression
is too strongly fixed

when confronted with evidence
of another direction
of illumination
we must make
some mental adjustment

it may be a simple one
or it may require
definite effort
and it may produce
pleasant
or unpleasant
reactions

one may be confused
while remembering
the original situation

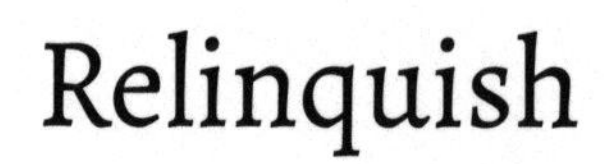

Relinquish

the Sky

Daylight, No Grief

Hail, holy Light, offspring of Heaven first-born!
—John Milton

Of firsts and beginnings, light knows the most. In its primary, faint motion of micro-tremor then radiant turn, swelling with uplift and slight ecstasy, it is light that knows all true names.

To seek out origins and their progressive trajectories, we have taught ourselves to investigate the phenomenal rays of long duration from star swarms and curling celestial storms, translating the myriad intensities of their transmission into timelines, elemental compositions, interior tectonics and churn. We peer into the sun's blinding recesses and can reasonably conjecture at a massive discharge's origins down to the finest shred of its first instant. We attune ourselves to light's potencies and emerge otherwise. With *insight*. We know.

I began my inquiry into light, simply: can I decipher a similar capacity to translate and speak the light with my living human body?

And by doing so, can I relinquish the intensities of an inherited orphan grief?

To speak with light is to encounter the trace of the originating mother body through its lost child. An orphan being, the light reaching us is jettisoned without turning its head back home. A constant flight...of some varieties in duration or decay, but ever onwards and with consistency in its appeal. The steadfastness of its message across vast spans remains nearly uncorrupted, and we look back through its narration into a body that is no longer there.

Oh tell us where you came from. Tell us of that body, its home.

My intuition told me that by confronting this originating, orphan phenomenon fully—by admitting its potencies, its possibilities, to transmit into and transform me—those aspects in me that were steeped in abandonment could be relinquished and freed. As an evaporation, a total admission into the sky's aerial, benign intelligence.

I want to inhabit that day.

A Slow Turn and Sash

No ghosts, sigh. No ghosts, move into deep blue ((sky)) → complexity. Aerialize grief with the uneven tempo channeled through your body—from sole to crooked knee, hold in the waist and elongate your spine, a far wrist now unfurling. Magnetize the white tongue: it flickers into light.

No ghosts, fly. Outrage and out pour, in staccato then languidly. No shush. Does she pull the redblack sleep of rage from the earth. Yes. Magma thorn through the whitecloud body. Some flesh and flay. No cry, but light. A flicker into. Light then light.

((series of hands, digitized
((some are so greatly pixelated
((they are nearly indecipherable

no ghosts, pain ((light)) no ghosts, pain

((but light——————>>

no ghosts, ((pain)

(light) light

Light

(A Method)

But because they may conduce to farther Discoveries
for compleating the Theory
especially as to the constitution
of the parts of natural Bodies,
I have here set down an account of them.

To render this Discourse short and distinct
I have first described the principal of my Observations
and then consider'd and made use of them.

The Observations are these.

A Broken Link in a Chain

> North Korean propaganda reveals "the orphan to be the national symbol of North Korea, the figure, it seems, most capable of being revolutionary. After all, just as the orphan is a broken link in a chain, so revolutions seek to create a radical break with history."
>
> —Clare Callahan, Duke U. Human Rights Archive

This pains me to read. My father, my mother, the various people I loved—they have had written into their spirits this un-requitable break. Reft from ancestors, family, homelands, and languages, these orphans populate my spirit. And I of them, too. We have cut and swung out at each other and at ourselves in the way we reached for that space inside, caving in. I swell with a novel vacuity, such bright black, quiet eyes.

There's nothing romantic about an orphan. If quiet, it is because they have perhaps learned to silence themselves before their hunger. Do they dwell interminably at a loss? We move onwards, but doesn't the content of our abandonment—this jettison—remain interiorly, always the same? An isolation. A dystrophy. What has been orphaned in me?

Where's the chain that lashes at this throat of history? The torn throat that fails to sing. To break from, to swallow without enunciating. To turn aside in the dust and moan.

I am going to have terrible, consequential dreams.

Touch the Black Magma Inside You

am I prepared

No beginnings as all beginnings. The greatest beginnings.
To sow in flames.
How the body bleeds. To staunch a wound—is fire the only salve?

When you burn yourself, the body holds the heat inside for days. Oh that blistersome heat. It scorches, even after the ice packs, cold compresses, the gauzy salves or pursed lips in their loving, cooing administrations. To feel a sun press through you in the middle of the night. To have it murmur against your body while you turn in your sheets, the windows wide open and crickets churning in the grass. Let. Me. Sleep.

to ride a hysterical horse into the sea

He lifted up his shirt. Fat, bubbly blisters like plastic packaging populated and pocked his back. *You need to go the hospital immediately.* The largest were as big as quarters. *I don't know how it happened.* I want to cry at how they softly—quietly—cling like gossamer barnacles to his skin. My hand coils tight against my side. I can't breathe.

Yet The Grief Body is a Body of Water

floods the chest cavity, up through the throat—an upper limit against which to speak is to drip. with breathless pressure, fulfilled in a black, still well. matte blur of its solitary reflected star. saturated intensities, to inhabit this *is to be inhabited*. a possession in silence. without break.

that she drowns in a black well alone. nameless composition of wet stone walls penetrate and hold. mother body, of first fluid movement in bright red isolation now blued. mother body of grief. of containment of hermetic chambers what light what light what light.

((pale)) sound—in small duration and stretch.
can she speak. no.
(pale) hand in longing.
can she reach. no.
pale. wan. silent. cold.
no. no. no. no. no.

A Slow Turn and Sash

You who have scattered
flower petals today
with your song,

Rightly serve the bodhisattva
as a favor to the spirit
that guides brightly and far
—translated by Bekhyon Yim

From Bekhyon:

In 760 AD, April 1st, two suns appeared and persisted for 10 days. The king was advised to find a loyal monk and have the monk make an offering with a prayer to chase away the chaos. The king made an offering and asked a monk who was passing by for a prayer. The monk said he will compose a Korean song called 도솔가.

This song, 도솔가, is also called 도살푸리 or 살푸리. The myth of multiple suns appearing simultaneously is prevalent in northeast Asia, popping up everywhere from Borneo, Mongolia, China, Korea, Japan, Tungus, and it usually refers to the chaos caused when the rule of a nation is up for grabs with several contenders. In Korea, this myth first appeared in the B.C. era.

Of course, there is a different origin explained to me by a monk in a cursory manner. 살푸리 or 사푸리 means releasing or setting free (푸리) of death (살 or 사). After harvest, farmers would burn the fields as a pest control measure to ensure that the crops grow healthy the next year. To minimize the unintended victims (insects and animals) from the fire, farmers used to put out sweet foods just outside the perimeter of the field that was set for burning in order to lure the insects and animals outside the fire zone.

> Because the practice was designed to save lives of these beings, it was called 살푸리.

To witness a 살푸리 is to observe a magnitude in motion. A meditative solo dance performed with a long white sash, in 살푸리 the figure rotates slowly on the balls and heels of the feet, often while extending the arms, stepping fluidly and flicking the sash with abrupt focus and grace. A dance of healing traditionally performed by the community shaman (무당), it discharges personal, familial, environmental, and social illness into the atmosphere through the fluttering sash's permutations in the air. The dance also releases the 무당 from the perilous energies channeling through her body in the service of the afflicted.

A poem. A dance. And the light was brought down.
I, too, would like to call down the light and be healed.

Breaks and Continuities

When I think of breaks in a chain, my mind can't also help but turn to wonder at continuities, at streaming extensions that *failed to break*. My imagination turns to light.

When I study satellite images of deep space that have been re-rendered to highlight their anatomy, I'm struck by how much data is carried in light. This image has been processed in order to make infrared information visible to us. From light, we can determine the composition of these celestial bodies, their rotation and movement, their age...we can even predict their futures.

((hi-res image of the Cygnus Nebulae))

radiation as light
heat as light
vibration as light
breath sky movement
how pause

All things in the universe transmit, casting informational streams from themselves. What does the heat generated from my body say? What am I broadcasting at every quivering instant? And the light that reaches me and interacts with my body, my perceptions, my ideas. What information is being so blindly delivered into me?

This orphaned light, jettisoned from a *distant*.
It never touches back or communicates with these far origins, but runs rampant always onward from them. No tethers, but darts.

precise nameless flowering
blank clover
onward
any attention
thin hand reaching into space

Northern Light

From 2015–2016, I traveled in sub-arctic and arctic coastal environments in order to observe strong variations and durations of light. I traveled in the fjords of Norway, into the arctic circle, and meditated alone in the howling blue-white expanse of Iceland's northwest fjords and frozen plains.

I was anonymous and alone, among kind but ultimately indifferent strangers. I often spoke to and saw nobody for days.

(fjord waters lap at a rough gray shore)

Our bodies require light.
I seek the opening of an understanding.

What is being said and said again with me. What am I now saying, too.
If my skin werecomposed of eyes, what would it see. If my body were a gigantic listening drum, what would I perceive. What do they want to pour into me.

A Monster

> By degrees, I remember, a stronger light pressed upon my nerves, so that I was obliged to shut my eyes. Darkness then came over me, and troubled me; but hardly had I felt this when, by opening my eyes, as I now suppose, the light poured in upon me again.
>
> —Frankenstein's Monster

dapple
flicker brook & stream

gold green soft curl
fern shook

Namelessness is another way of inhabiting my body without intentions. The green ferns of the forest floor curl gently as I walk past, indicating to me how we are the same. Sky folds miraculously, reappears in the breaks between young oak trees, dappled maple shade and blue. Silence and softly. A doe and her fawn emerge to observe me. We stand momentarily apprising our bodies, the shared way we inhabit the space around us in that instant. A flick of the tongue and they sink back into the hill. Small charm of the brook as it rumbles earnestly over crayfish and softened stones. My hand glides across rock lips, gathers on a mossy face as I kneel down.

I knew, and could distinguish, nothing,
but feeling pain invade me on all sides,
I sat down and wept.

(Don't or Fail to) Touch the Black Magma Inside You

I'm incapable of so much.
I pull away from the fire though it desperately wants to lick my skin.
My arm, just under the elbow—at the most tender pale spot—
flushes deep red.
I touch it with flattened fingers. No marks.

Light fell so obliquely on the Air
it seemed in that place of contact
to be wholly transmitted
in the rough concave
of a prismatic hand.
Yet little or no sensible Light
ought to be reflected from thence.

Like a black or dark spot inside the body
this pressure set loose Arcs.
These Arcs increased and bended
more and more
till they were completed.
Circles and Rings encompassing.

I Relinquish a Mother, Inside

It flickers, this pain, when it calls to me by name. He whispers to me, but right now I am only able to speak the matte black language of lead. What is asleep inside and where is its home. *I can't account for the things I never had.* I feel him reach towards me—his desire is soft, endless, earthy. His hands sweep slowly across my arms, my forehead, stomach, hips, and sides. Why does "welcome" require using your arms? He presses me to his chest firmly, hands along my back. *I must account for the ones I abandoned or lost.* I smell cedar.

An unfamiliar space. Without longing. I want to get inside this feeling and recalibrate my ability to recognize a new way of being "home." Dark stars move through my eyes. I keep them wide open, observe the flecks of light reflecting from his.

Afterwards, I turn aside on my pillow, eyes clamped tight, transforming the white lamplight into a speckled night sky that falls down across my face, my mind.

I can't remember very much from that time. Images appear to me like badly exposed film stills, or as though I am hovering high up above them and peering down. Certain details are clear—a glint of light off a building at noon. Strangely, *I see myself* in these memories. I was not at home in my own body, but dwelling elsewhere. I hang over my own head, recall the stove, my desk, the bathroom mirror and the neighbor's patio outside.

thin streak of sunlight on the pale wooden floor	despondency

A Slow Turn and Sash

I spoke briefly with a Sami resident of Tromsø, Norway, who informed me that the northern lights could be controlled and made more energetic by standing beneath them with a white sheet.

I feel certain I am on the right track.
I move slowly through the hoarfrost.
I wander off the trail.

How One Comes to (Not) Know Light

Ansel Adams, *The Negative*.
Gaston Bachelard, *Air and Dreams. Also Water and Dreams.*
R. W. Ditchburn, *Light*.
Robert Hooke, *Micrographia*.
Sir Isaac Newton, *Opticks*.
Marjorie Hope Nicolson, *Newton Demands the Muse: Newton's Opticks and the 18th Century Poets.*
Mary Shelley, *Frankenstein*.

One Sky, One Sea

While in northern Wyoming, the spare quality of the grasslands and the dynamism of the mountain ridges rising up in all directions reminded me of Iceland, where I spent the month of February. The blonde, silver, matte green and gray shades that dominated the environment when I first arrived mirrored the close-of-winter hues populating my visual field outside Reykjavik and along the mouth of the Snæfellsnes peninsula.

These similarities, however, make me particularly long for the way Iceland's snowy landscapes in the upper mountain ridges and plains held the light—my time in the west fjords of Norway are deeply ingrained inside my body, now. The immense saturation of blue at the cusp of nightfall holds the sky with a heavy physicality. The horizon disappears, and distances recede into you with profound intimacy.

I drove across the inner mountain plains of the Westfjords of Iceland and snaked my way alongside the central fjord to arrive in Norðurfjörður at the close of day. I had arranged to stay in an abandoned bookstore in Flateyri, a village just south of the fjord. Flateyri is notorious for having the highest incidences of avalanches in the country. The wind howled down from the high mountains towering over the village. A few tall streetlamps illuminated the iced over street with a gaseous yellow haze.

My Icelandic host left her shift briefly at the cannery to unlock the door for me. It was actually her son's apartment, but he was in the capital for the weekend. Covered in what looked like Tyvek overalls, she looked at me with bemusement when I asked for a restaurant nearby. It was late February and nearly 5pm. The wind screamed between the ice glazed houses.

"The gas station at the end of the street—they'll have something. But they close soon. There is nothing else open here. Nothing."

I drove the half mile there; I didn't trust myself to not slip or make the walk over the iced streets in time. When I walked in, a petite Filipina woman was working the register. We both startled at each other.

"Why are you here?" she gasped at me. I was wondering the same thing about her.

Her eyes gleamed with a sudden wetness. I saw what I infrequently see in other Asian women's eyes when we encounter each other in various abandonments. Kin.

"I'm a writer. I'm here to study winter light. What are you doing here?"

"I got married. I moved and had a son. And now I work."

The short aisle had chips, crispbreads, tins of sardines. Pasta sauce. A freezer of curry boxes. I bought two cans of Gull beer and sardines. She smiled at me with such longing. I wanted to ask her more about her life.

The high ice cliffs around the village loomed over us, even in this small shelter.

I didn't know how to proceed.
This isolation. It devours.

A Slow Turn, No Sash

Holding a metal bowl of clear water in both hands, he looked skyward before tipping it into the ground. So wracked in knots inside, clear water is a simple gesture that speaks beyond his stuttering ways. It hardly splashes as the yellowing grass sips it up. *Make an offering to the sky.*

A single picture of my father's lost mother remains: white stoic face enveloped in the velvet black of a neglected history. Her eyes are not eyes to me, but dark pigments scattered on a page. I strain to see a body and not its representation. He walks back into the house five steps before me.

I observe his characteristically stiff gait across the flagstone steps, listen to no rustling wind. *This is how you remember*. Pour it out.

A Mother Body

Even if anyone heard, they would not come to help her.

Her father had beautiful hands. He was always making things.
She clings to them.
His face has been erased from her long ago.

And what else do you remember?
A frog. A little frog.

A "Monster"

There was one boy who was in clear distress. His face contorted with pain. No one stopped to even look at him. He walked about, holding his clasped hands up to his chest. I am not sure how old he was. Perhaps eight or nine. He was very small. The documentary was made over fifteen years ago. My spirit tells me this young North Korean boy did not survive. And when I think of this, I realize that the only documents that attest to his life could very well be the footage that was used in that film. And I was observing the recreated light patterns of what had once echoed off his body and into the camera's lens, captured.

Magnetize the White Tongue

Light flows through black streams to concourse with spiritual ecstasy. Lacking an equation for "nox," various mute horses guide us along the matte gray green sea. Distant bypass and veil. I wrote your name with birch tar fumes and yarn. It wasn't a story, but a feeling that flowed. Factually with reflection. Like snow.

My first encounter with the aurora borealis was dreamlike. I was in a plane headed into the arctic circle. Thick blackness descended into a sheaf of noctilucent clouds blanketing the earth beneath us. They burned with a neon blue hue in a thin stream that ate all distances. I felt small and disembodied, aloft. I noticed a shimmering gray-green ribbon furling with digital consequence, moving distinctly but uncannily as though caught in a sputtering breeze. It streamed with impossible ephemerality alongside the edge of our flightpath to feebly drop as though failing into the glowing blue neon "sea."

"If you shake the white sheet, it will move, too...

after daylight has failed
the sun need may be considered

And then it will come down for you."

The Black Magma Inside You

After all. After all that. After tender pinecones. After gnarled roots gripping stone faces and treacherous scree. After vivid electric surges across the watery sheen. After lavender pale dusk of hours. After the dreamless sleep of day.

After distance. After the squall devoured the shore. After no gulls. After frozen waterfalls with broken teeth. After darkness. After all needle thin rays of starlight in a black gale. After lonely hoarfrost. After distance. After desolation.

What have I learned to say.
Can I say it.

제사
祭祀

waves or corpuscles

I wrote my dream on paper and held it up before the sun
admitting its gray blue rays to infiltrate the pale pulp
shielding the fixed quotient of my "asiatic" eyes
from soft burning white peerless day

my text was indecipherable to man
at such a distance and small in black curves
anointed only with care transmitted through
the bent dark rod of my spine shoulders length of arm and fist
curling in laborious dexterity to write

how my son likewise curved into my hand prematurely
his coal dark eyes wrapped with filmy gauze
swathed vaguely in gray and pale blue
thin paper lips left open a cry

when light congregated by a glass through which
the stormy noon of day in fire
took hold and spit forth black curling swarms
deciphering how the action between bodies and light is mutual

for is not fire a body heated so hot as to emit light copiously
and the power of each body lay in what separates
such diff'rent beams, each prismatic cell

some questions

can this be done
without delay

can one
admit dust

must all
remain separated
facing the same direction
resting evenly

must agitation
present a problem

difference is so little that it need seldom be considered

is a “well-executed sequence of actions”
a necessity

Notes on the text:

Immense friendship and gratitude to Marthe Reed, who is so deeply missed and loved, who published an excerpt of this collection as a chapbook with Black Radish Books. My thanks to Julia Cohen for printing "The Thaw" in the Fanzine, and to Cream City Review for publishing "a pale saturation (in day." And lastly, my deep gratitude to Stephen Motika, who saw what I was pointing to, and everyone at Nightboat Books who thoughtfully labored to give this work a beautiful home.

I composed the primary materials for this book while in residence at Kunstnarhuset Messen (Ålvik, Norway), Hafnarborg (Hafnarfjörður, Iceland), and UCross Foundation (Ucross, Wyoming). I spent the summer of 2014 in Norway, where the intensely long summer days over the fjord infiltrated my body. I am terrifically indebted to the program administrator Ingunn van Etten for selecting me for the program, my hosts Simone Hooymans and Hans Pulles, and the kind denizens of Norway who welcomed and sheltered me—most especially Bjørn Otto Wallevik, for his kindness, generosity, and human goodness. His friendship was a soft light that fell upon me.

I returned to Kunstanarhuset Messen for winter a year later, traveling briefly into the arctic circle in Tromsø, before heading to Iceland. I wanted to engulf myself—not just in the long night and its subtle stars, but the light captured in ice and glaciers. There is perhaps no adequate language to describe what I uncovered in the recesses of my spirit there—in violent stormy darkness, under the needle thin rays of crystalline stars, beneath hundreds of feet of glacial ice, or quieted by the digital finesse of the aurora borealis. This book, along with my various video pieces, represent my best efforts to share.

My thanks also goes to the Pew Center for the Arts and Heritage for a 2013 Fellowship award, which gave me the latitude to travel and steep myself in these considerations, and the Alliance of American Artists for support so I could stay at UCross Foundation while I incubated the immensity of these experiences. The Pew Fellowship encouraged me to pursue new opportunities and challenged me to grow in many ways, some quite radically. I am also grateful to the University of the Arts for financing my winter travel. I am especially thankful to Christa DiMarco, who made me feel instantly at home, Niles Lewandowski, who encouraged me, and most especially Michele Kishita, who has become a dear spirit friend and inspires me to see the world with joyous eyes. Knowing her is one of my greatest pleasures.

I consulted and excised from several texts which are named in "Relinquish the Sky." Some of these borrowed texts appear in greater profundity than others. I willfully appropriated primarily from men who are canonical in their fields...I felt that giving my ideas equal weight within their considerations and discoveries re-centered their methods—which are predominantly phenomenological—in my body and history, to open alternative pathways for the human pursuit of knowledge. I also wanted to highlight the immense insights and poetry of their writing, which I frequently found intensely beautiful.

Sueyeun Juliette Lee (이수연) grew up three miles from the CIA and currently lives in Denver, Colorado. A former Pew Fellow in the Arts for Literature, she also makes video and installation art. Find more of her work at silentbroadcast.com

NIGHTBOAT BOOKS

Nightboat Books, a nonprofit organization, seeks to develop audiences for writers whose work resists convention and transcends boundaries. We publish books rich with poignancy, intelligence, and risk. Please visit nightboat.org to learn about our titles and how you can support our future publications.

The following individuals have supported the publication of this book. We thank them for their generosity and commitment to the mission of Nightboat Books:

Kazim Ali
Anonymous (4)
Abraham Avnisan
Jean C. Ballantyne
The Robert C. Brooks Revocable Trust
Amanda Greenberger
Rachel Lithgow
Anne Marie Macari
Elizabeth Madans
Elizabeth Motika
Thomas Shardlow
Benjamin Taylor
Jerrie Whitfield & Richard Motika

This book is made possible, in part, by grants from the New York City Department of Cultural Affairs in partnership with the City Council and the New York State Council on the Arts Literature Program.